The

Empty

Bed

The
Empty
Bed

RACHEL HADAS

Wesleyan University Press
Published by University Press of New England
Hanover and London

Wesleyan University Press
Published by University Press of New England, Hanover, NH 03755
© 1995 by Rachel Hadas
All rights reserved
Printed in the United States of America
5 4 3 2 1
CIP data appear at the end of the book

ACKNOWLEDGMENTS

Most of these poems have appeared in periodicals, sometimes in slightly differ-
ent form, as follows: "Faultlines" and "Nine Tiles," *College English*; "The House
beside the Sea," "Literary Executor," "Black Lullaby," and "Song," *PN Review*;
"Lunch the Day after Thanksgiving," "Spring," and "Mars and Venus," *Southwest
Review*; "Alternatives," *Harvard Magazine*; "Lower Level EE" (here titled "Lower Level,
Room EE"), "Winter Night" (here titled "Through a Glass"), and "Peculiar Sanctity,"
Western Humanities Review; "Benefit Night, New York City Ballet," "The Friend,"
"Lullaby," "April Heat," *The Formalist*; "Orange," *Boston Review*; "Six of One," "Frieze
Advancing," "Passage," "A Glimpse of Simon Verity," and "The Last Movie," *The
New Republic*; "Thank You and Goodbye," "Sleepy's Entrance," and "Upon My
Mother's Death," *Threepenny Review*; "The Bees of the Invisible" and "The Hinge,"
Paris Review; "Arguments of Silence," *Yale Review*; "Recoveries," *Kenyon Review*; "Black
Wings" and "Lullaby," *Raritan*; "The Red House" and "Four Lives, Stirring," *The New
Yorker*; "Coleman 1445," *Poetry New York*; "May," *The New Criterion*.

As well as to the dead who are commemorated in its pages,
this book is dedicated to three among the living:
my husband, George Edwards, our son, Jonathan,
and my friend Kathy Janowitz,
who helped me shape the manuscript
into its present form.

Contents

I

II

III

I

Faultlines

Cracks and fissures: are these an illusion
or is it an illusion
that somehow someplace whole is where we live?

Everywhere, deep gashes and connections.
All over the city, bagged
sleepers huddle on benches,

bundle in doorways. Morning light
pries and prods the hugged
body in its pink quilt.

I know the fissures.
Soaping my son's back in the bath I touch them,
not scars, not bones, not visible, but lines

of cleavage. Battle lines.
In rooms all over the city
catheter pumps beep, blink a red-eyed warning,

so many bats, so many kindly ghosts
dripping survival out in gouts of time.
Saturday mornings, boys bounce in from soccer.

Discontinuities, thumbed references:
I strain across the numb abyss as if
wholeness were givable, were within reach.

I wait beside the fountain.
The bells of the cathedral bong out spring.
The faultline means that time is working wrong.

Lunch the Day after Thanksgiving

To my right (your left) the steamed-up pane
doesn't quite hide a line of hungry would-

be lunchers who gaze meaningfully in;
to my left (your right) low November sun

has just transformed a red and blue plaid elbow
into a radiant morsel of stained glass

seen out of the corner of my eye
as happiness always is.

I thought it was the slant of autumn light
cleaving the fuggy room that pierced my heart,

but it was something simpler. It was sky.
When nothing else but appetite is left,

will each of us softly shut her story's door?
When appetite itself (look at today)

is sated? Putting down your fork, you say
one struggles to . . . something about control.

Squinting at the sun, I nod, half-listen,
and wholly disagree. Some things are wrested

from us for nothing, service on the house,
whatever we may feel about divestment.

Hunger for daylight: would you say it slides
off to one side like a book from a sleep-numbed hand?

I think it dogs us up to the last moment.
Reluctantly we stand up and prepare

to leave the table to that bright-eyed party
watching us through the window,

breathing dense plumes into the afternoon.
Or we could sit and sit.

If we sat long enough the light would redden,
oh burdened vessel chugging out of port.

Alternatives

Our argument went walking down the street.
Fresh light bounced off the water:
a harbor was behind us, out of sight
except for these exuberant refractions,
morning's hope and afternoon's late ripeness

arm in arm. What time was it? Where were we?
I craned for street signs; could decipher nothing.
Radiant, rinsed, the slates beneath our feet
shone up at us, wet silver.
Was this the city where we'd always lived?

Spring

Here come the new pastels! Magnolias fling
their pink hearts wide, forsythias explode.
Winter's subterranean fires accede
to spring.

If I were in this picture, would it be real?
inquires the child, observing a black border
between the worlds. It garbles sunlit order.
Grass, crocuses conceal

imperfectly an energy that sleeps
through months of cold and every April stirs.
As if on schedule, I hear her curse
the kids whose shouts have woken her. She leaps

from her dank ambuscade,
roused from hibernation by their play
who cower, whisper, giggle, run away.
She shuffles back to the rag bed she's made

under a bench. Next my father's ghost
observes the children seesaw, swing, and climb.
Silent, he calls "Be careful!"
                              What's the time?
Dazzled in gritty sunshine, I have lost

the thread, can only grope at doubleness.
Spring greenery is no
less real for being so
thinly spread. The black beneath the grass

pulls at the children shoving at the sky.
Winter's secret melts. I am restored.
Hard spring light pours down without a word
into the pure, the newly naked eye.

April Heat

Having waited for today,
all blossoms burst, a mass of white.
Yesterday you came back to town,
riding the crest of sudden heat.

I can't help thinking *One more spring,*
reentry, a reprieve from death . . .
This year I freshly take it in
and so can see a bit beneath

the sullen surface day by day —
allowance, deadline, expectation,
furrows of work and glints of play,
and the rare flag of celebration.

I welcome you, but I cannot
speak for you, or ask the reason
for your return to this vast nest.
Spring can be a wretched season.

You come; magnolias explode,
birds hurl themselves across the sky
again — the while world's that one word.
Perhaps you have come back to die.

The city's an immense machine,
multiple layers for living in
gaudily now festooned with green.
You stand at a gateway marked *Begin*

and do not look to left or right.
Friends can gesture, nothing more.
The season holds its thrilling note.
You put your hand out to a door.

Lower Level, Room EE

Hospital, prison, leper colony,
country of the dead,
all tropes for institutions on the border.

The border has become an institution,
a place of walls. It's no coincidence
this white room has a door for in and out

but not one window where the gaze may wander
in an abstraction half involuntary;
no hazy hinterland where faces beckon,

relatives signal, and acquaintances
wave; no landscape of the in-between.
Still, EE's soundproof door lets people in

and who comes here moves like a messenger.
A mother. A canary in a mineshaft.
Basket of sunlight and the beams leak out.

Cup dipped down to catch a sip of ocean.
Glass held up to capture bright blue air.
Love's ladder of illusion, rung by rung.

Through a Glass

(i) *The End of Summer*

Slicing through summer's intricate frail web
meant to have paced the blade of contradictions.
Sun lights up a cobweb of connections.
I think of you; am hurtled at a pane
of glass. Blood, crazings; then these symptoms ebb.
Were they in fact part of the barrier
beyond whose glassiness I couldn't see?
Trying to reach you where you live again,
I witness life take place within the frame.
A tall man stirs a saucepan, silently
spied through a pane. What's cooking? Stormclouds gather
dark at the horizon where a grim
force like a fist is squeezing things together,
uncritical, gigantic, blind: a mother,
if all this longing really leads back home.

(ii) *Winter Night*

Unhuggable, unspeaking. A new year
exacts its toll, the January cold
twisting the dial of urgency. The old
preoccupation; a new undertow.
Nausea, pain, impatience do their dance.
Several more syllables could be tapped out:
boredom, disgust, abstraction. And fear,
through whose low fog, clinging and venomous,
I flap a hand as if to try to clear
a space between us. "Put some music on

to fill the silence," maybe I should say
as silence settles deeper, dark and glum.
No drawbridge I can manage seems to span
the moat of the grim fortress you've become.

The End of the Tunnel

After a spell of waiting,
a corridor of wind.
Then wailing like a blizzard,
whining, blowing, blind.
Through walls of white and silence,
arrival. Lamplight slices
woods that grew here before
I blundered into this
wildness that will grow tall
without me. Shut the door.

Inside by the fire,
I'm still in the cold wood,
buffeted and spun
by skirling winter winds.
As one door slowly closes,
another's opening.

Gospel of entrances!
A shape of living flesh,
the offering of whose body
I carry on asleep,
awake, and never thinking.
Under the brick, a key.
Under the shirt, a shape.
Weariness seeks a refuge
from the weight of winter.
Mourning peels the scenes
of life's activities
in strips from cold partitions
so draughty channels open
to the courageous stranger.

Icy currents lift
and for an instant hold
thin veils floating
out from a wall of stone.

The House beside the Sea

I wore that fiction like a fine white shirt
And asked no favor but to play the part.
—James Merrill

Like a fine *what* shirt I put it on,
the house beside the sea,
enclosing like a tangy honeymoon
the fiction of a place for you and me?

A fine white shirt.

White? Without my eyes I couldn't see.
I merely felt the shining of the sea.
I have no eyes or teeth, but I can hear.
Are those gigantic scissors near my ear?

Snip. Snip. Snip. Lock hell.

Hell is locked out, I know it. Thank you, though.
No one is here in this salt bungalow
but me, I think. And you? Could you be there,
swathed in the sheer white scrim of ever after?

Snip. Snip. Snip.

It takes no eyes to sense
something is cutting at the final thread
that ties us two together,
keeps me near the salt blood of the sea.

Lock hell.

The house that locks hell out,
the house hell locks me into,
the house of hell? And yet
I'm glad to be alive here.

                    Snip. Snip. Snip.

No eyes, no taste,
only ablution (Keats's reverie
of pure ablution round earth's human shores)
or threadbare fabric of another day;

                    a fine white shirt

clutched at and held, survival's jagged tear,
the house beside the sea,
the radiance of vestments that we wear,
rags of the robe unraveling in salt air.

Chiasmus

We are comparing notes on honesty.
"Only if I love someone can I

summon the guts to speak the truth," I say,
and offer nervously

"I guess that's normal." "On the contrary,
people confide in strangers," you reply.

So that it's to their loved ones that they lie?
is my reaction (uttered silently).

Reading the stifled thought, you glance at me
fondly, wearily, illegibly.

We all are implicated either way,
your muted gaze both says and doesn't say.

Benefit Night, New York City Ballet

Once in its mannered mode
the dance appeared to me
a dusty stiff brocade
of faded mystery.

But this was years ago.
Later it came to seem
a vain if gallant blow
aimed at the cruel regime

of time and gravity
by beauty to defy
the merciless decree:
we grow old, sicken, die.

The years that press us down
carve sullen masks of age.
Eyes fixed on the dim ground,
we creep across our stage.

Now sitting here with you
in the enchanted dark
I still hold to this view.
The sweating dancers work

lightly to lift a great
somber collective pall—
mortality's dead weight—
from you and me and all

who, separate, doomed, and dumb,
can drink in nonetheless
our share of the sublime.
The dancers dance for us:

our grief, love, vanity.
Their bodies form a screen
between humanity
and the pull of the unseen.

The burdens we all bear,
great or small, find ease
this evening in the sheer
radiance of disguise.

For as we raptly gaze
at limbs in cool blue light
sculpting a carnal maze
of intricate delight,

of passions sketched on air,
it is ourselves we see,
divested of despair.
You turn and smile at me.

The Friend

Late August; early afternoon.
Already windfalls have begun
to stipple ditches red and green.
An object like a fallen leaf,
foreboding autumn leitmotif —
tawny toad on deep green lawn —
huddles and hops and then is gone.
And summer's last soliloquy:
a new-fledged Monarch butterfly
glides to a silent halt on me,
uncurls its tongue (long, sticky, black)
to give my leg a gentle lick.
Its wings, still wet, they are so new,
wave tentatively to and fro.
Weightless, it preens upon the knee
of this unwieldy human tree,
balancing stillness and delight
for minutes, hours . . .

                    Already night
and time to take a stroll, the full
moon spilling silver on the hill.
Dirt roads gleam pale as desert sands
and moonbeams carve mysterious bands
along each blanked-out meadow, lawn,
and flowerbed.

                    And cut to dawn.
The eyes I open closed upon
visions that charmed sleep's somber room
into a garden whose rich bloom
took on shapes of human faces.
Here were embarrassments of graces!

Crivelli's focus, Cezanne's heft,
Van der Weyden's gorgeous weft,
Modigliani's oval fruit,
Vermeer's ponderers of light:
from these I waken, pull the shade
up on their question.

                                              Art is made
and then what? Given, traded, lent,
brimful of nonsense, deeply meant?
What covert message is conveyed
in every brushstroke's private code?
Even as I wave sleep away,
these puzzles glint at me today.
For August like a burnished knife
has pierced a layer of drowsy life
and rivulets of language flow
beneath the world I think I know.
Images sticky with dream-fog;
love's interrupted dialogue;
the moon-drenched radiance of last night;
all gave a sleeper food for thought
about the tendrils of connection
between this season and affection.
Don't objects in late summer light
look double: self and opposite?
Shadows that heighten sunshine's glory
also tell a darker story
as misty mornings need more time
to burn off into clear sublime;
as afternoons of lustrous gold
yield earlier to dark and cold.
As — cozy, equinoctial —
summertime subsides to fall,
my thoughts again take up one strand
whose knotty texture forms a bond
from now to — who knows when? Beyond

this August haven, this plateau,
how will the conversation go?

To build it up has been a long
and tender process. Speech and song;
absence and presence; what is dreamed,
remembered, improvised, and schemed,
combined to build a dwelling we
have entered intermittently
for two years now; no, more than two.
And all this time the thought of you
has been a part of what I do,
imagine, feel, especially write.
You stimulate each appetite
(the best sauce, hunger) like a ghost
presiding over moments lost,
recalled, recaptured. And this sense
of getting back experience
fills me with the same unearned joy
as if a life were rerun free.
I feel released by you: to play,
mourn and rejoice, to laugh and cry,
dear friend who's stepped out of the sky
as if to keep me company.

Company. It's one great theme
of poetry — affection's dream.
Out of mutual isolation
we're drawn into a confrontation,
two people pulled each from their place
toward one another, through a space
that may be empty, bleak, and sour,
may be a garden in full flower.
Season of spiders, fall demands
why we fling these wistful strands,
this chancy web of frailest thread
spun from affinity or need

to bridge the shadow chasm of
our mutual requirement: love.
Either emotional plenitude
moves us still nearer to the good
or else the pangs of vacancy
urge us toward proximity.

Why should we measure psychic weather
just because souls are drawn together?
It makes a difference because
art and love have separate laws.
To get beyond the lonely self,
both of them reach across a gulf,
reciprocally operating
to praise the scene of their creating,
salute their source of consciousness.
Art with serene obsessiveness
takes in the world's variety,
discharging it as poetry.
Love with opposing appetite.
basks in a world of dual delight.
One feels in loving less alone,
my heaven-sent companion—

which is no reason to confuse
a human presence with the muse,
says common sense, which adds *Give in
to ordinary life again.*
And with September close at hand
I have to heed this cold command
and shut your lovely face away.
With your mortality at bay
as if it were my own, I start
to raise a wall around my heart
in time for school, where every book
will render back your questioning look.
Behind each page I try to teach,

I'll sense you slipping out of reach.
Slowly as in a dream of fear,
deeply familiar, deeply dear
friend, you drift, you float, you glide.
Stranded on the season's side,
I stare until my eyes are sore.
I stare till I can see no more,
then turn to winter's lexicon
and try to write our friendship down.

II

Sleepy's Entrance

In memory of Gregory Kolovakos

A flashy sign whose loud red upper case
proclaims a store for mattresses and beds
on a second floor on Broadway and Seventy-Second Street
is also announcing a new way
to slip out of the city, of the bright
bustling world of waking.
Hot, tired in the taxi coming home
from Gregory's memorial, I can't
remember having seen this sign before;
register, rather (as someone might note
a new place in the neighborhood to eat)
one more portal.

        "I'll be out of this
soon," said Gregory the last time we spoke,
as if "this" were a specially tedious
master's program or an airless room.

I didn't understand. For what had winter
ground us down to, me and many others,
if not sleepwalkers trudging in the deep
trenches of habit? Only now and then
did someone break the rhythm, crane a neck
backwards to gawk up at the blandly backlit
screen of a sky that somehow lay behind
the dull quotidian air. Only rarely
did anyone seem to spot a Sleepy's Entrance.

Thank You and Goodbye

In memory of David Kalstone

Thunder stalks the darkening rim of sky
this afternoon. A twittering alarm
in the sick maple means that birds and noisy

red squirrels are sheltering from the coming storm.
Twilight, evening, night . . . and fitful lightning
restlessly pulses. Put the light out; drive

with headlights off — still, darkly, you can see,
cannot *not* see. They tell me our friend D
lay all his final day and night and gazed.

Stroking fingers, cooling cloths
over his forehead could not shut his eyes.
Did ending's imminence compel the vigil

or did the hours of vigilance spell death?
Friends who, waiting by the bedside, held
his hand and said *Relax* and said *We love you*

did not themselves relax. We call it watching.
Nearing the end, one feels the need of portals
to mark the passage. But how to get through?

Etiquette dictates *That was delicious*
when what we mean is *Take my plate away.*
Thank you edges over to Goodbye.

28

The Bees of the Invisible

In memory of Dan Conner

A golden haze — departed souls —
hovers above the summer lawn,
performs its barely legible
dances inside a mote of sun.

Hovering above the summer lawn
wordless graffiti of unease
dance inside a mote of sun
and disappear into the trees.

Wordless graffiti of unease
when people die where do they go?
disappear into the trees.
I'm not sure I remember you.

When people die where do they go?
Summer stormclouds drift away.
I'm not sure I remember you.
You've left, but here's another day.

Summer stormclouds drift away.
The sky is blank but beautiful.
You've left, yet here's another day,
a cup of emptiness to fill.

The sky is blank but beautiful.
Nothing will ever be the same —
a cup of emptiness to fill,
symbols shaped into a name.

Nothing will ever be the same.
I cannot mourn without a sense
of symbols shaped into a name,
alphabet of intelligence.

I cannot mourn without a sense
of something that transcends the whole
alphabet of intelligence,
the bees of the invisible.

Black Wings

"You look up at the sky, down to the ground,
and there is nothing to say," my friend remarks.
No, accurately describes the aftermath
of his announcement of a sudden death.

Well, yes. My vacantly globe-girdling gaze
hangs in the gap between two outstretched black
wings that (though no two people give them one
epithet) we both can recognize.

I look unseeing up, where he has looked.
The warp is working. Something curdled, thick
coats our parted lips. We name no taste
but circle like conspirators around

a pitiful ailanthus, chopstick-thin,
scanty concealment, feeble Birnam Wood
against the unseen, loudly marching army
drumming on the door of the horizon.

Yet as disguise the tree is a success.
It hides us not from the still uninstructed
boy at our knees who bounces his bright ball
against a brick wall, but from one another.

Call it a focus, axis, mournful Maypole —
I'm thankful it is standing here between us
as something flicks past our averted faces.
We stammer words out hopelessly as laws.

We crane our necks at nothing but an absence.
The city simmers its brew of births and losses.
A dark air brushes past. We breathe an edge
of wordless agitation on the wind.

Coleman 1445

In memory of Michael Pelonero

I would like to tell you what I saw,
but it's not easy. I don't know its name.

I was in the presence of transition.
An arch, a rope-bridge frail above sheer space.

Between what stations did the thread of breath
tremble and heave beneath its mortal burden?

I squeezed a hand. Strong hand, big bones, long fingers.
Heard, low, "I'm hanging in there." This was true.

But whether clinging to the ropes or dangling
from the slick rock-face matters only now

that I have left the room in whose still air
one recognizes passage and no more.

The rope bridge swaying over emptiness,
the arrow of blind noon, went either way.

While I tell this, my stored tears do not
fall so much as hang, globed goblin fruit

gone in an instant. But that strenuous room,
the crux of struggle, had no place for them.

Again the spotlight of some massive fact
strokes the stubble of a gasping breath.

A cistern fills, but no one has the key.
The tank of tears will burst unless I say

what it was I saw,
the name of which I tell you I don't know.

The Last Movie

In memory of Charles Barber

Saturday, April 5. Welles's *Othello*:
black and white grid of rage,

steam of sheer fury spewing from the vent
of violence that followed where they went.

Wind howled on the battlements, but sun
gilded glum canals. The lovers floated

beneath black bridges, coupled in stone rooms.
The unrepentant villain (at the start

so all the rest was flashback)
dangled from a cage

squinting inscrutably at the funeral
procession winding through the town below.

The air was full of wailing.
Knives of sunlight glittered on the sea.

We lurched out onto Fifty-Seventh Street.
You said "I think I'm dying."

Next week your eyes went out.
Shining under the lamp,

your blue gaze, now opaque,
your face drawn sharper but still beautiful:

from this extremity you can attempt
to rise to rage and grief. Or you can yield

to the cozy quicksand of the bed.
You wave your hand at walls of books:

"What do I do? Do I throw all these away?"
Their anecdotes, their comforts — now black glass.

The Wolf in the Bed

In memory of Charles Barber

From when you still could see,
do you remember the print beside your bed?
Doré's "Red Riding Hood":
the wide-eyed little girl
shares a pillow with the bonneted
beast. Recall the sidelong
look that links the child
and the shaggy monster
snuggling beside her.
Blankets pulled to their chins
conceal the tangled matters underneath:
a secret region, shadowy deep forest
through which a covered basket
is being carried, bread and wine
and books to the sick one's bedside.
You are the girl in bed beside the beast
or you're the grandmother, I visit you —
but no, since it's my mother, too, who's dying.
Is she in bed with you, since both are breathed on,
crowded, jostled by the restless wolf?
Now I arrive and climb in with you both
(the wolf makes room for me a little while)
and gingerly, so as not
to jar your various lifelines,
cradle you in my arms, my friend, my mother,
and read you stories of children
walking unattended through dark woods.

Leftovers

That was the spring I squatted on two floors,
gaping at the bright interiors
of twin refrigerators left forlorn
in widely separated parts of town.
These gleaming dual criteria of lives
halted halfway through milk or mayonnaise
(lives not yet ended, moving day by day
out of the realm where calories hold sway) —
neither held much that anyone would care
to eat, yet neither one was wholly bare.
Food had become irrelevant, a key
that opened nothing useful. Presently
both heavy doors shut. Some days passed. A pair
of sisters tackled what was waiting there.
One came down from Maine to see her brother,
one from New Mexico to help her mother
(I, on the spot already, made one other).
To see, to help — or simply to discard
some dubious pudding? That part wasn't hard.
Each fridge was empty soon. Much else was not.
Leftovers aren't all liable to rot.
Every item that we threw away
was matched by others proof against decay,
papers to study later in the frame
not of a freezer but of human time.
Meanwhile as margarine, cottage cheese, white wine
went into the garbage, down the drain,
other displacements also now kicked in.
A pair of people were reduced to skin
and bone; then bone; then ash; then thought alone.
Yet myriad clues about them all the while
had waited patiently in drawer or file.

Now one refrigerator was trucked off,
the other filled with alien foodstuff.
But there remain the fragile-feeling leaves
traced with the many mappings of two lives.

Upon My Mother's Death

In memory of Elizabeth C. Hadas

The empty bed. And instantly I knew
and also didn't, as I do
and do not even now

where she had gone
precipitously, leaving me alone
to telephone

and do whatever else had to be done.
First, for example, furnish my ID
lest some impostor claiming to be me

should grab her few belongings; next, take them
in long sealed boxes home (but now whose home?);
and last myself continue to become

her who was gone.
This gradual process had been going on
for all our two lives' simultaneous span

but now I lifted her
once chunky person, feather-
light abruptly now, henceforth, forever,

ferried her backward from the empty bed.
Where? Anywhere instead
of that pristine dominion of the dead,

straight to the corridor
where chatting nurses eyed a visitor:
would this belated daughter shed a tear?

No. Yes. No. Yes. Then I absorbed the sense,
the respite, brief and sweet, the recompense:
living, to love the quick and dead at once.

Deciphering this later, I read 'lose'
for love — a logic I dare not refuse.
Love lorn live lose lone: need we really choose?

As when I wrote of C "Your absence walks"
but later read it as "Your absence works";
both ways mean a blurry sleeper wakes.

Again, C, dying, left some books to me —
or was it "lent" them? Generosity
either way you read it — legacy

stretching across the boundaries of love,
defying the short time we're let to live,
the scanty sum it's possible to give.

Only for grief is our capacity
limitless. Illegibility
has a silver lining, I now see.

It blurs the limits of mortality.

Missing Lines

In memory of James Turcotte

As years accumulate
and pile up into stacks,
the heap of one's omissions
teeters to fearful heights —
tales in the telling glossed,
names garbled or forgotten,
whole seasons of connection
for whatever reason
not communicated, therefore lost.
Negligence, indifference,
the weariness of habit,
that strangling shawl
grief wraps around itself,
the monitory knot
tightened to crippling noose,
the pointing finger bloodless,
numb with the nevermore —
All knots, untie!
Open up! Admit
James, whom I had left out.

From your hospital bed
you telephoned past ten o'clock at night.
Urgently you asked "Am I too late?"
Too late for what?
The burning question
proved to be technique,
haiku or sonnet,
whatever formal framework could encompass
the crucial axioms you were working out,

also the simple fact,
but luminous, that you
had lived, were living still,
and thinking about space
(your last two poems
you'd illustrated: galaxy, black hole).
We conferred over the phone, your lips
dry, by the sound of it,
and your mind racing, pen
too, to take it down
while there was time.
ABAB, I dictated. Like this.
Or it can also go ABBA.
And you who'd shrugged off rhyme
as a harsh master, or irrelevant,
asked me to repeat the way it went.

You had been ruddy, sturdy, fair,
a salt-and-pepper blond with flecks of grey.
Now gaunt and golden-haired,
your eyes new, bluer, deeper:
this was how you looked to me last week.
Metallic sutures on a patch of skull,
every kind of line,
of character, in bones or poetry,
too strong and clear not to be followed through
even at this late date.
I must leave nothing out.
Am I too late?
Failed affection is a precious cup
I try to rivet now,
seeing again the staples on your brow.
Time, if there is time, will fill it up.

How many messages we speak, send, spill
daily! Innumerable
lines blurred like ink,

like letters running down
envelopes carried foolishly through rain,
spatters of repetition wearing thin
the very point we meant to hammer in.
So with the dialogic poetry
of all the lines that flashed from you to me
and back again — only belatedly,
even involuntarily,
after our final conversation
I trace, grasp, see them.
Cheekbones: bronzed knobs of pain.
Skull they opened to let poison in.
Azure eyes, restless, scanning for a sign.

Was it a mordant graduation
gift for the earnest student you'd become,
that after years of arguing
poems and stories in a basement room
you were rewarded by this elevation —
twelve stories up, a room to call your own,
the magic laptop
lent by Sloane-Kettering's librarian
propped across your thin
knees in a bedroom golden with spring sun?

The Changes

The dead are doubly changed.
Above them pale disasters float,
coronas of remembrance.
They are not demanding; they can wait
while with no choice we fumblingly take in

not only who is now
walking the earth, but how much room they need.
We have to learn strange indirections, new
ways of communicating with the dead.
And there are other alterations:

firm features blurred, but granite the long gowns,
motionless, hanging, every fluting clear,
immutable as words
angry or kind engraved upon the air,
susceptible of no revision there.

It's fortunate the dead become so slim!
Not a day goes by
you do not occupy
my heart. The task, it seems,
of autumn is to shoehorn legacies

into a house, a head's restricted space
and somehow go on living in the place
not cramped or weighted, stifled or pressed down.
If people could be tactful as their books,
our dead, leaving the bereaved alone,

would wait till they were needed, only then
opening to spill out joy and pain.
While time, although intangible as air,
can drag us down into despair,
words go right on working. Sane, immune,

they keep their heads and call the tune,
blessed in this precious quality
of self-possession, gravity,
the patience of storage, keeping where
nothing can wake them till we choose to hear.

Radical compensation!
Weakening, fevered, thin;
tentative touch against the weary skin;
and then farewell, the bone
reduced to ash alone,

that final transformation.
Or should I say translation?
Dear heart, most cherished ghost,
what is beloved for beauty, not duration,
and so is learned cannot be wholly lost.

Hence this paradox:
your secret self—each glum or hopeful mood,
wretched or radiant, dreaming of the good,
of joy and friendship past or still to come—
is fragile as a leaf of onionskin

or shut up in a box
And yet not so! The ash,
scattered to earth, nevertheless floats free
into the breezy unaccountability
of air. So whether weightless or dragged down,

love persists. Or first one, then the other:
I can lie back in dreams of you and float,
then bathe in tears. Pleasure and pain, to plumb
the depths of memory. Then the daily dumb
withholding when the silence starts again,

caught in whose pendulum
first I believe in emptiness
as screening the beloved presences
and then quick as an eyeflick change my mind,
contrarily convinced we must be born

already used to loss, renunciation —
so numb we seem, so ready to give up
we scarcely sense the second when the live
creature vanishes. And day by day
helpful habit deepens the divide

till a dichotomy
opens between the living and the dead.

The Double Legacy

Something is wrong with our lives here.
Books make this groping thought come clear
as they declare
for a world elsewhere
with joys to discover,
wrongs to right,
where lover and lover
unite forever
amid celebrations
for restorations
of what was lost.
How modest the cost
of using one's eyes!
Look at the page,
abandon age.

If years bring stale accumulation,
stories offer a simulation,
hopeful and fresh
as a birthday wish.
Your heart is sore?
Read some more.
My mother's dead;
but in my head
are words she said
from books she read,
patient, dumb,
ready to come
to life whenever
I broach their cover.

Nor do I mourn her death alone.
Six weeks later my friend was gone —

his young strength quenched, his beauty cut
off like a flower at the bleeding root.
I followed feeling, found instead
a double spectre, an empty bed.
For my mother and my friend
the summer brought no happy end
such as we find upon a shelf.
But closure can extend itself
from the safe haven of a page
into our world of loss and rage —
the world in which my friend left me
love in the form of poetry:
eleven cartons from his collection,
volume on volume of affection.
These treasures salvaged from the wrack
cannot bring the giver back,
but in our narrow human scope
are still my best, my only hope
of repossessing all that he
was able to pass on to me.

As for my mother's legacy,
it can't be told as quantity,
piled up or counted or assessed.
If right this minute I should divest
myself of all that can be seen
in what she left me, there'd remain
hours upon hours of gentleness:
her reading voice's calm caress,
the realm of books she opened to
my young attention as I grew
and let me roam in, safe and free,
with a whole world for company
of voices I can always hear
whenever no one else is near
or when I'm reading to my son
and so can hand affection on

in the same shape as what I took
so happily from her: a book.

Last month, one cloudy afternoon,
we spread her ashes on the lawn.
I think it was that night the moon
shone not on one more desperate dream
but on a half-deciphered scheme
of secret balance — loss and gain
with love their fulcrum, love and pain.
The world was torment; also feast.
There was no choice: partake, digest.
Two lives I loved are now compressed
into this whiteness, paper-thin
but mercifully written on.

My mother and friend have no more need
of books — at least the kind we read.
But if, like loved books, they survive,
what else but love keeps them alive?
Memory, attention — atmosphere
libraries offer everywhere
together with the admonition
that touches on mankind's condition,
our blessing and our punishment:
nothing is given; all is lent.

I do not give, therefore, but lend
books from my mother and my friend.
Affection's double legacy
provisionally passed to me;
I pass it on now to this library.

Holiday Movies

"Dracula" and "Aladdin" share a theme.
No, more than one.
Confinement first, in magic lamp or tomb
strange creatures issue from —
genie or vampire, bottled energy,
fierce appetites for all eternity.
Then metamorphoses:
the desiccated count who stealthily
licks a wet razor dry
can unpredictably
transform himself, whether to a baboon
or to a soft-eyed swain.
The virgin typist, tightly corseted,
rigid at her machine,
sprouts fangs, proceeds to scream
for babies' blood. The genie,
genial heretofore,
turns threatening suddenly,
a tall cerulean thunderhead, as dire
as his new master,
the sorcerer hankering for power, more power
who's finally trapped inside
the deadpan little lamp forevermore,
or the equivalent (remember
in these stories nothing is forever).

I lack the quenchless thirst,
the weird exuberance
either of the urchin whose strong will
and mother wit prevail
or of the undead,

though locked inside my head,
cramped, transformed into a little room,
they can be found, all my beloved dead,
once here and now inexorably gone.

May

As soon as the cold old sun feels warm,
a powerful impulse says *Lie down.*
Down on a bench; in the lap of noon;
on the green bosom of a lawn;
down on a hillside, under a tree,
in mother's absence. In or on,
horizontality's all one.
Effaced each spring a little more
by being forty-two, three, four,
wrapped in invisibility,
I lie and look across the sky.
Near the horizon a streak of green
swells like a harbinger of dawn —
not green like new leaves everywhere,
rather a verdant atmosphere.
I tilt my face, luxuriate —
chin up and eyes shut — in the heat,
warmth that this year feels different.
Spring means all it ever meant,
but the earth where I lay my head
covers my two beloved dead.
They do not say "Forsake the sun."
They say "We loved it, and we're gone."
That golden magnanimity!
Ten minutes is enough for me.
Opening my eyes, I readjust
my mind and body. For I must
gradually as in a dream
return to vertical again,
stand up and somehow move beyond
my buried mother, my buried friend.

The Rinse

Rags soiled with various
leakages, mud, blood:
I press and wring and scrub the rusty
margins of overflow
and think of diapers and chucks and changes.

Two springs ago a pair of people lay
who now have changed themselves, have turned to soil,
no longer soiled or soiling, spilling, spilled,
no accident to mop, no spoon the numb
fingers cannot carry to the face.

Recoveries

Sweet Briar, Virginia, November 1992; Alsace, pre-1924

A college pool, central Virginia.
The octogenarian who swims next to me
for half an hour at noon each Saturday
recalls Olivier's confiserie,
the best in Strasbourg when he was a boy.
"Et ceci se passait dans des temps très anciens,"
is what I'm briefly tempted to reply,
having been translating Victor Hugo
today. "This happened very long ago."
I smile and nod and kick and swim away.
Delicious smells and tastes accompany
me along the warm blue shimmering lane.
Cream and butter, chocolate, raspberry . . .
Can such rich pastries ever be again?

460 Riverside Drive? No time

The old apartment's empty, dingy, brown,
Riverside cum West End cum nursing home.
Dressed in khakis, weary, old, and slow,
my long absent father's back in town.
He and I meet by appointment here
to go through papers? Books? It isn't clear.
We want to chat, but we've forgotten how,
so many years have passed with him away.
And time is running out. Tomorrow we
must go our separate ways forever. Oh,
I babble, let me go and buy some snacks —
horseradish, kippered herrings, bagels, lox . . .
I try to think what other foods we shared.

He tries to smile at me. He strokes his beard.
Without a word, we both have taken in
we'll never have a place to live again.
The acrid desolation of the dream
is tangy as a herring packed in cream.

Greenwich Village, mid-1950's

Once upon a time near Union Square,
but I will never know exactly where,
high in a loft recorders used to rest
carefully sheltered in a tall fur nest.
These recorders' pale red-headed owner
taught recorder to my elder sister.
My new friend, a painter, knew this teacher
because she studied Plato with her lover.
For this recorder teacher had a lover —
an actress and a Holocaust survivor
and a Greek scholar, and a scholar's daughter.
I was the little sister. I remember
standing shyly waiting in the foyer
studying the wood of each recorder,
soprano, alto, bass. Mouthpiece of amber?
Blond wood or dark? The fur (wolf? fox?) was silver.

St. Luke's Hospital, May 20, 1992

Hurrying to the hospital last May,
late in the afternoon, a lovely day,
I slow down slightly to admire the sky.
Mommy is tired; she can wait for me
a few more minutes. Because yesterday
she liked a coconut Italian ice
I bought her on the corner of Broadway,
I buy another. Lemon is my choice.

I walk and lick; she'll finish it. We'll share.
Her illness is not contagious.
I reach her room and nobody is there.
The bed is empty and my mother gone.
Unnoticed, melting lemon leaves a stain
on my jacket. When I take this in
later, the sequence plays itself again:
the stroll, the sweet, the blankness at the end.
If I could make this melting come undone,
would I have seen my mother one more time?
If I clean my sleeve, do I erase
my final expectation of her face?

23 Waverly Place, June 1992

About to ring the bell of a good friend,
I encountered Richard. In his hand
was a plastic box of candied ginger.
He held it toward me with a courteous gesture,
munching meanwhile. Nodding toward the door
of the apartment I was aiming for,
he raised his brows and queried "How much more?"
"Bad," I replied. We didn't speak out loud.
I took the proffered candy, sucked and chewed
its fibrous sharpness. Nothing more to say.
We sketched a wave and then both moved away,
he to the elevator, I the door.
No surprises waited for me there.
I knew beforehand how my friend was lying
disoriented, feeble, blind, and dying.
Each visit was a vigil. So I sat
taking in the candied ginger's heat.

Coda

The future's where we place our hope and fear.
What's done is done. The past cannot recur.
Anecdote, dream, and memory all refer
to experience no longer there.
Yet look at what is rising through the air!
Fox fur, ginger, melting lemon ice
successively appear. Can we live twice?
Is nothing lost? I reach a new conclusion:
leave the future to its own confusion.
My business is with what I find I know
through story, memory, dream. Since this is so,
I am a vessel full beyond the brim
even as life leaks out, a steady stream
of losses running toward oblivion.
But how to make one's daily life maintain
a balance between plenitude and pain,
such fullness and such unremitting waste?
Ginger offered in an outstretched hand.
A blond recorder resting in its stand.
Kippers. Pastries. A remembered taste.

III

Literary Executor

Unfinished business — order of the day.
A decade's papers filed away,
bedded in a wooden chest
for hibernation, at least
until some snooper finds the key.

Then the dead letters wake. They play,
sob, snicker, flirt outrageously
before subsiding in their nest,
unfinished business.

Dreams that fade back into the sky,
old quarrels between you and me
leave us delighted and distressed.
Imperfect dawns light up the east.
Incomplete sunsets flood the west.
No closure — this is poetry,
unfinished business.

Peculiar Sanctity

*". . . the tradition which affirmed the
peculiar sanctity of the sick, the weak, and
the dying . . . perhaps came to an end for
literature with the death of Milly Theale."*
— Lionel Trilling, "Mansfield Park"

Except it didn't. It went underground
as some diseases have been known to do,
returning with a vengeance in our time.
To note the renaissance of elegy
as the defining genre of our day
is not to claim for form
merely the reflex of a pendulum
stupidly swinging. There are differences.
First of all, a fierce self-righteousness
beats its drum through our diffused distress.
Secondly, people take enormous pride
in giving utterance to grief and loss.
It is as if we shoved huge stones aside
to make room for our little threnodies.
Silence is shameful, more than shameful, death.
Is speech not life, then, animal instinct,
survival's automatic pilot, breath?
No; it requires courage. Thirdly, though
for silence and for speech the penalty
our plague exacts is utterly the same,
we are supposed to rage, seethe, overflow
with fury; brandish, not just grief, but blame,
level reproaches at the government.
How could so many be allowed to die?

Fourthly, it is not correct to say
"I'm dying of"; one says "I'm living with,"
thus adding to the gallantry of myth.

In mortal sickness, courage is no lie.
With or without peculiar sanctity,
people have always managed as they could.
And once the sick one takes the downward road
to that broad region shrouded in twilight,
similarities with those before
become more marked than differences of mode.
The figures look the same: tall Tenderness
bends by the bed to offer a caress.
And everyone who passes or who stays
must grapple with the place's doubleness:
the tremulous wish to live at any price
versus the drawn-out longing for release.
When what the scourge can do is done at last,
the bystanders all having done their best;
when everyone's acknowledged this to be
something not curable by elegy
(silence is death, and so is poetry),
they rise, go out, and seek the light of day
for a little while. They turn away,
yes, but only for a breathing space
from the old, new, peculiar sanctity,
before returning to their grisly task.

Lullaby

I wept, then slept,
in mourning for
mortality — who knew?
An air caressing and uneasy both.

If all the pain could be spun out to song
calm as the breathing of a child asleep,
the long savannahs of desire, despair
caught in the slumberer's damp hair,

I would sustain these pressures with a hand
held up as to ward off
the entrances, the echoes,
the enemies of quiet in the house.

Orange

When it is time to begin to think of dying,
nothing is too minuscule to mourn.
In my case it was freshly from the fire
I stumbled into winter, shut the door,
and lying back, a Lady of Shalott
to my own life, gazed out at a procession
threading the pallid January hills.
But at the edge of vision something flashed.
An orange tablecloth hung on a line
rigid as a sheet of frozen fire.

Rage's ringmarks on the tree of life
ask to be etched forever. Failing that,
color takes up where characters leave off,
pays its homage to the draining glass.
The tomcat stayed out first for one night, next
two, then a week, and finally was clean gone,
swallowed up in summer's greeny gullet.
Already we forget the way he looked,
doubt his existence. But the orange pelt
ignites its emblem in the mirror's eye.

Nine Tiles

A painting by Sylvia Benitez

I see! I recognize
infections of fever and desire.
The stranger captured, painted them as fire.

The story of the fire told again
more eloquently this time by a white
witch — not told but crackled at white heat —

cools to a husk, collapses in a false
stillness, as if every wound were salved
smooth each time the smoky tale's retold.

Visibly the fire burns to myth.
The ashes sinking sift symmetrical
patterns, articulated into order.

The threefold world is multiplied to nine
panels, as etiquette with sovereign gesture
apportions envy, mourning, greed, delight

each to its own compartment and perspective.
Bird, cross, corpse, ladder, coil of snake or hose
quenching disaster but itself a portent

of worse to come; the white involved with black
inextricably; windows in the wall
that also face the world. The buried corpse,

unquiet in the garden's scorching soil,
resurrects as bird of deadly omen.
The breasts and penis of a man turned woman,

red, raw, cry FIRE FIRE
transfixed in the hot vision of the painter
who, stranger to another's history,

is privy to the desperate and dire,
palette knife poised to a pulse of sheer combustion,
the crosses on the floor tiles spelling D A N G E R.

Frieze Advancing

Whether the moving figure keeps both hands
concealed beneath the folds of drapery
or briefly stretches one long finger out
(gesture both hard to read and quickly over),
to misconstrue the meaning spells disaster.
Should I step forth as to reciprocate
conjectured greetings from a formal face
already turning, wholly turned away,
or block the onward path by kneeling down
in homage, or, a more ingenious thought,
twitch that stately progress to a halt
by grasping at the corner of the cloak?
Fugitive gleams of recognition jell
into a brisk admonitory wave,
or an abrupter flapping, chopping motion.
But does it warn or beckon?
Does it mean "come closer" or "keep off"?
Cautiously construing any sudden
gesture as camouflage, I keep my distance
only to notice how I've stumbled in
between the cracks of limit. As I watch,
the figure moves along what now appears
a predetermined path with steady pace.
But what such onward motion signifies
is eloquently wrapped in reticence.
These even footfalls, this steadfast refusal
of any least temptation to look back:
stoicism or stolidity
grapple as motives with a silent fierce
glee at the achievement of escape.

Six of One

To know the difference between full and empty
doesn't get easier. Take menstruation —
fullness a falling follows.
Or take the long-illegible sonata
slanting at last like lightning through a screen
but also herald to the lash of rain.
So late acknowledgment and so desire
painted my face.

        There was a corridor
smelling of paint. Walk down it to the end.
Open the door. Enter the empty room.
But then it seemed I was the empty one —
I who had scraped my brainpan gourd-seed dry,
my shining face the pane for light's invasion,
my parchment skin the January mirror.

The Hinge

Resentments of grown children: slanting, thin,
grudging like a peevish autumn rain.
Reproaches we all visit on our parents.
The teller on the couch
reeling out old grievances
with practiced fluency is less resentful
than the upstanding orphan resolutely
refusing to find fault
with the unforgivable
death of his mother. Listen.

Wordsworth writes of his mother at a slant,
rather refers than mourns. Thus: "Early died
My honoured Mother, she who was the heart
And hinge of all our learnings and our loves."
Warm beating center, then, and also that
which folds so things pass through. The son continues:
"She left us destitute, and, as we might,
Trooping together." Beggars on the road?
Brood of the mother hen mentioned a few lines back?
And where in all this is the father? Absence
shadows the story. "Little suits it me
To break upon the sabbath of her rest
With any thought that looks at others' blame."
Who *are* those others? Wordsworth shakes his head,
discouraging conjecture as he opens
the door a hairsbreadth further to admit
a crack of light. For, his lips pursed, he adds
"Nor would I praise her but in perfect love.
Hence am I checked." Yet he goes on from there
"In gratitude, and for the sake of truth,

Unheard by her," to thoughts akin to thanks.
Correcting what ghost voices?
Answering what reproaches? Made by whom?

Then Henry James upon his mother's death
when he was thirty-nine: "She was our life.
She was the house, the keystone of the arch.
She held us all together, and without her
we are scattered reeds." Not destitute,
trooping together—this time strewn apart.

Whether of straggling children or sad adults,
the legacy is desolation. Whether
our mothers and our fathers live or die,
but more especially when they die, the sin
is unforgivable. I blame the one
for dying too soon, leaving a poor troop.
I blame her in the sabbath of her rest,
deaf to her son's periphrases, resentments.
I blame the absent father for his absence
if he was absent—worse if he was present.
I blame the other mother, full of years,
for letting slip the keystone of the arch.
And when we're done with blame, reproach, resentment,
the creaky hinges of the heart can open.
In the artists' colony, it's winter.
A writer's mother sends from California
boxes of scarves for all her daughter's colleagues.
A father sends a box of Clementines.
My mother sends me out into the snow
in silence where I listen for her voice.

Passage

Tracking what is mortal, we forsake
    the past, keep chugging in
    our children's foamy wake,
        snatch at sleep,
        grumble at Time's
appalling leakage from the hourglass.

Rhyming relentless chronicles of loss
    (love sent us here and back
    to love we hope to go)
        provides no
        barricade
beyond the fortress of a lamplit room

nor is there any haven except sleep
    against the outer dark-
    ness into which we plunge
        nightly, that
        never lasts:
comes the miraculous renewal, dawn.

Over the bleak debris of cancelled things —
    diminishing, erased
    in each passenger's wake —
        one breath's blown
        at the abyss.
A thin song rises to the lips like air.

Song

Even if every summer past were calling,
    fingers of recognition at the stretch
        waving through cloud,
how much more delight could be allowed?
    How far can gesture reach
        when every moment you are falling, falling?

The mode is elegy
    in whose red light somehow you walk
        forward and also
glance backward as you go.
    When friends bend near to comfort you with talk,
        is it inevitable that they lie?

Not that I could remember or defend
    just why I love you. Possibly
        the way that we refuse to sacrifice
the rendezvous of eyes,
    or that with sudden snorts of laughter we
        puncture the pompous zero of an end.

Arguments of Silence

(i)

Silence as friend. For what can grow without it?
As enemy. For we know what it is said to equal.

If silence equals death, does death equal silence?
Necessary condition, not sufficient.

Only in the charged silence after death
are certain voices heard, while the chat of the living

dwindles behind an invisible veil or glaze
or curtain that may rise to further speech.

(ii)

Silence as style, as stubbornness, as stoical
courage, expedience, patience. Or as fear.

"There's nothing more to say," and walked away.
But how do I know what's there until I say it?

The impulse swells, as fountains do not stop,
as pressure building causes corks to pop:

74

new takes, new combinations. Or not new
but as my lips interpret an old law.

I salute you, friends who would not button
your lips but kept them, chapped and bloody, open;

who refused to huddle caged as in contagion,
forced to find your balance from between

the horns of the dilemma how to live
at once outside and inside of your bodies

and dance and balance not struck dumb by fear,
your voice a thread, your proper labyrinth's clue.

That certain words are tinny in our time
(*recovery community denial*

culture diversity even maybe *silence*
even dare I breathe it sometimes *death*);

that speech is not always heroic, not
always interesting or necessary;

that silence is as likely to mean sleep,
exhaustion, or discretion, as death

doesn't release us from the snare of language.
True, wives and husbands, children and their parents

know without speaking what is wished or meant —
the curse of family life, and the reward.

Habit, telepathy, passion:
nothing exempts us from our chatty birthright.

The danger's hardly tyranny by silence.
It's hard to shut us up while we draw breath.

If anything can guarantee our silence,
death can. But silence doesn't equal death.

Lullaby II

As if there were no enemy,
evening rocks me into sleep.
Tomorrow's possibility
undoes the bodice, lets me breathe
out, in evenly. A deep
valedictory sobbing breath
commemorates a span of time
gone as if it had never been.
Yes, we bravely resist the new.
But sun, moon, the beloved's name
we exile to oblivion
and do not speak of all we know.

Histories of ups and downs,
of arguments and stillnesses
cast shadows on the wall of days
silence envelops here, as snow
sifting into a hollow place
erases what there was to see.
Memory rising in the eyes
peaks to knowledge and subsides,
leaving a wash of images
stranded like seaweed at low tide.
We recognize this dear debris
and do not speak of all we know.

A Glimpse of Simon Verity

The master mason perches on the scaffolding,
wool cap askew and stone dust in his hair,
his wiry torso bare,
chisel and mallet chipping at a figure
not fully formed, emerging from the stone.
Mauve October twilight, greenhouse-warm,
holds us. The hospital where you were born
is a mere stone's throw (limestone chip) away.
You have just fallen up a flight of stairs
and grazed your knee, but now you dry your tears
and watch the face the mason's hands awaken.

Mars and Venus

(*Botticelli, ca. 1475*)

Gold tape gently billowing with her breathing,
triple V's at bosom and sleeve and ankle
point to partings, leading the eye to where her
                         body emerges.

Wait: This painting is an enormous V-ness.
Look how unemphatically, almost absent-
ly her left hand seems to be plucking one more
                         labial gilded

entry between her waist and her knee. Reclining,
she becomes a series of languid valleys
who herself creates an entire other
                         landscape of V-ness

in her consort. Slumbering, numb, the war-god —
head thrown back; neck, shoulders, torso open —
seems oblivious equally to the lady
                         and to the satyrs,

naughty toddlers, trying on Mars's helmet,
blowing conches into his ear, or crawling
gleefully through his corselet, their behavior
                         an awful nuisance

all for nothing. Here in this vague green valley
lamb and lion, love and war are united
by indifference equally to these babies
                         and to each other.

Do the little faunlets call Mars their Daddy?
Either way, his answer is not forthcoming.
Drained by amorous combat, the god is elsewhere.
                            Vigilant Venus

gazes, not at him, nor at us, but rather
seems the merest eyeflick away from over-
seeing Sandro putting the final touches
                            onto his family

portrait: Mars and Venus, it's called. Or Father
sleeps while Mother's keeping a watchful eye out
not on the children (*are* these the couple's children?)
                            but beyond; elsewhere.

Violence sleeps. Desire is in need of further
sustenance: her V's are unfilled, her fingers
seem to press, to promise, half hiding, showing
                            translucent treasures

he has seen and savored to satisfaction.
Rhyming, secret, intimate, and familiar,
their two mysteries mingle in this: deferral
                            of ever after.

Four Lives, Stirring

Lemons on damask (one).
Curve of a gold-framed mirror
reflecting blackness. Also black, a squat
empty vase, or maybe bowler hat.
Drained seltzer siphon; shallow teacup (two).
Oblong cake tin. Furled fan.
Enamel coffee pot with pinks, carnations.
Pink-lipped conch brimful of filtered sun.
Lavender linen tablecloth a woman
stretches her arm along
(three) and lays her cheek
against her flowered sleeve
while massive fronds and beanstalk stems of green
climb the far wall. Two women
face each other (four)
across an empty table white as milk
(marble? formica?) lit by a square of window.
No, they are not quite facing one another.
The one in the green turban,
on the far side of the table, faces us
but sits a little skewed from her companion,
as if to shrug off
a relentless gaze, probe, accusation—
that back turned toward us, we will never know.

Surfaces, decorations, interruptions.
Starched white damask. Smell of lemons. Coffee
and wine displaced by cut
flowers in decanter, pot. A drowsy hour
at noon. A downy cheek.
Tulips keep their red or yellow glossy
under a mantle of snow.
Daffodils poke gallantly from sleet.

Under the flowers, vegetables, and fruit
offering their faces to the day
is secret cold, a hidden core of white
concealing in its turn the warm black blanket
that under the eye-aching
brilliance of March shrouds everything that might,
that will strain towards the light.

Black Lullaby

Aeneas dipped down underneath the lake;
black bullocks drugged and slaughtered one by one
as in a dream nudged compasses awake.
Where were they? Birdless world where no sun shone.

Black bullocks drugged and slaughtered one by one
whose blood cemented an important spell.
Where were they? Birdless world where no sun shone
and every gesture was centripetal.

The blood cemented this important spell:
unscramble order. Cleave the dark lagoon.
If every gesture is centripetal,
dive for the center, the dark city, dawn.

Unscramble order. Cleave the dark lagoon.
Head for an isle of voices. Always keep
in sight the center, the dark city, dawn,
and gazing at them sail away to sleep.

Envoy

Each giant form lounged on its pedestal,
reclined to metaphor, remade the stage.
Their voices sounded brute, antiphonal,
numbly nostalgic for a golden age.

Unfolding images remade the stage.
Tiptoe we climbed the monumental stair,
showered by voices brute, antiphonal,
and suddenly emerged to outer air.

The Red House

Malevich painted you. Can I come in?
I'm on the outside, floating in the void,
trying to name what curdles (milk? wheat? cloud?)

and laps at your foundation like foam.
You have three small white chimneys but not one
window, unless your windows face the sea,

if that is sea there. Lighthouse; tower; friend
planted precisely where the black horizon
unrolls its ribbon under pasty sky,

I wished to settle all
accounts and shut the book.
No, reach and never turn the final page

where—sturdy, pokerfaced,
sunset-stained to russet—you were standing.
I had walked toward you through a wolfish wood.

I had swum a shark-infested sea
to reach you at that edge
where human constructs dwindle to a verge

and questions like who made you,
responsive to what vision, when and why,
evaporate to mere biography.

But on that day
when my lips and hands stop skittering
and they can scoop my vision of the good

out of its hidden niche behind my eyes,
I hope you, tall old house, are what they see,
silent sentry at extremity,

facing the uneasy elements,
your eyes, your windows shrouded with salt spray,
or windowless but still awash with light.

UNIVERSITY PRESS OF NEW ENGLAND

publishes books under its own imprint and is the publisher for Brandeis University Press, Brown University Press, Dartmouth College, Middlebury College Press, University of New Hampshire, University of Rhode Island, Tufts University, University of Vermont, Wesleyan University Press, and Salzburg Seminar.

ABOUT THE AUTHOR

Rachel Hadas is a professor of English at Rutgers University. Her many published works include *Living in Time* (Rutgers, 1990), *Pass It On* (Princeton, 1989), as well as *Slow Transparency* and *A Son from Sleep* (Wesleyan, 1983, 1987). Her poems and translations have appeared in *The Atlantic*, *The New Yorker*, *TLS*, *The New Republic*, and *Grand Street*, among others.

Library of Congress Cataloging-in-Publication Data

Hadas, Rachel.
    The empty bed / by Rachel Hadas.
       p.   cm. — (Wesleyan poetry)
     ISBN 0–8195-2221-X (cloth). — ISBN 0-8195–1225–7 (pbk.)
    I. Title. II. Series.
   PS3558.A3116E47   1994
   811'.54—dc20   94–24100
  ∞